ROUSSEAU

STILL VOYAGES

CONTENTS

Painting on Cover: *Battle of a Tiger and a Buffalo* (1908)

Graphic design: Sandra Brys

First published in the United States in 1995 by Chelsea House Publishers.

© 1989 by Casterman, Tournai

First Printing

1 3 5 7 9 8 6 4 2

ISBN 0-7910-2816-X

Art for Children
ROUSSEAU
STILL VOYAGES

By Didier Grosjean & Claudine Roland

Illustrations by Francine De Boeck

Translation by John Goodman

CHELSEA HOUSE PUBLISHERS
NEW YORK • PHILADELPHIA

Fireman? Airplane pilot? Astronaut? Football player?

I was 11 years old, and I had to think about my future. Did I want to be president? A juggler? A businessman? A frogman?

What were my abilities? What was my psychological profile? Should I be a tractor driver? A race-car driver? A journalist? An economist?

What decisions! My sister was too young to worry about such questions. I looked at her and saw her making fun of me—that made me mad.

But suddenly she became serious. She came toward me with a big book that Dad had just shown her. It was heavy, but she managed to lift it onto the table.

"When I grow up, I want to be a customs officer!" she said.

Customs officer! What was with her? She was only five years old and she already had some crazy ideas.

But the last thing to do was to contradict her.

The Snake Charmer,
1907.

I turned the book around to look at it. On the cover was a picture of a jungle and a mysterious lady with long hair playing the flute for several snakes.

The title was *Rousseau the Customs Officer.* I asked my sister some questions, and it was just as I thought—she didn't even know what a customs officer was! But she knew she wanted to be one. The book was full of giant plants, lions, tigers, and people being eaten by wild beasts. It was these images that had captured my little sister's imagination. What she really wanted was to be an explorer.

This came as something of a shock. An explorer! Why hadn't I thought of that! That's much more interesting than being president or chief fireman.

I felt what Mom calls a "jealous attack" coming on.

I got control of myself. After all, the fact that my sister had thought of it first didn't mean I couldn't be an explorer, too. It sounded great to set out in search of, well, treasure, or a gold mine, or even scientific data, if it were in a country like the one in the book.

What country was that? A hot country covered with strange plants and gigantic flowers, and with lots of lions and tigers. It looked like Africa. But then I saw a man with brown skin and feathers on his head struggling with a gorilla. Everybody knows that American Indians wear feathers like that. So was it Africa or America?

I had to stop and do some chores—what a drag! But the next day I'd find out more about this customs official.

Exotic Landscape, **1910 (detail).**

hat a day! My sister kept bugging me—she still wanted to be a customs officer, even after I explained that this Rousseau can't have been one because he was an explorer. Then, just before leaving for school, I asked my father some questions. What a disaster! With Caroline listening, he told me that this Rousseau had never been an explorer—he was a painter. It was a good thing he mentioned that Rousseau hadn't been a customs officer either, otherwise my sister's triumph would have been complete!

Myself, Landscape Portrait, 1890. Rousseau painted himself here at the Saint Nicholas dock near the toll house where he worked. Rousseau playfully depicted the rosette given academic prizewinners on his lapel.

The Toll House, undated. Rousseau here shows the fortifications where he must have often kept guard.

Photograph of the Saint Nicholas dock. Note the toll officers on the lower right.

When he wasn't painting, he worked at a duty house overseeing the collection of taxes and tariffs. Aside from that, Dad couldn't tell me much. He said that he'd read the book with the jungle pictures all the way through, but he didn't remember anything about it—when parents get old their memories aren't what they used to be. I asked him where Rousseau the tax officer had traveled to paint his pictures, and he told me that he'd been to Mexico, but that the trip was of no importance. Then he said that if I wanted to know more I should read the book. That was clever of him.

here are photographs of animals on the walls of my classroom. In fact, right over my desk there's an enormous tiger baring his teeth. At recess, I asked the teacher what countries tigers live in. I saw she was stumped, but she smiled and looked it up in the encyclopedia.

In Asia. Tigers live in Asia. Not in America, not even South America. How about that! Asia!

At home, my little sister was waiting for me, and she had lots of questions.

I don't like big books. I never have the courage to read them from the beginning, so I flip through them beginning at the back. That's what I did with this one, and I came upon a poem. It was by Guillaume Apollinaire, a great poet that I knew a little about. In school, when I was little, I'd learned five of his lines by heart.

With four camels in tow
Don Pedro from Alapalooza
Traveled the world and admired it.
He did what I'd like to do
If I had four camels, too.

So Apollinaire wanted to be an explorer! In the poems in the big book, he wrote about Rousseau and Mexico.

Rousseau in his studio.

The Muse Inspiring the Poet, 1909. This painting depicts Apollinaire accompanied by Marie Laurencin, an artist who had greatly influenced the poet. When Laurencin pointed out to Rousseau that she was much thinner than he had painted her, he answered: "Guillaume is a great poet. He needs a big muse."

You'll remember the Aztec landscape,
    Rousseau,
With its forests where mango and banana
    trees grow,
And monkeys spilling watermelon blood
And the white emperor who was shot there.
You got the ideas for your paintings from
    Mexico:
A red sun burnishing the banana leaves
And you, brave soldier, trading your
    military coat
For the blue jacket of a customs officer.

So Dad was right about Mexico. But the last line confused me. Was Rousseau the Customs Officer a real customs officer? If so, I didn't want my sister to know about it!

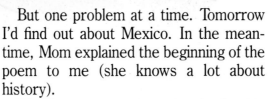

Napoleon III.

But one problem at a time. Tomorrow I'd find out about Mexico. In the meantime, Mom explained the beginning of the poem to me (she knows a lot about history).

The Aztecs were a people who lived in Mexico a long time ago. They're almost all dead now. In fact, "Aztec landscape" means "Mexican landscape" here.

As for the "white emperor who was shot there," that's Maximilian. His story is a sad one. It happened around 1860. France was then governed by an emperor named Napoleon III who wanted to establish an empire in Mexico. He sent a French army there, and he named Maximilian and his wife Charlotte Emperor and Empress of Mexico. But the Mexicans didn't like this, and things turned ugly. Maximilian was shot, and Charlotte went mad from grief.

A work by the great 19th-century painter Manet, *The Execution of Emperor Maximilian of Mexico* (1867–1868).

Maximilian and his wife Charlotte of Belgium.

Before becoming a tax officer, Rousseau must have served as a soldier against the Mexicans.

Fortunately, things didn't go as badly for him as for Maximilian, "the white emperor who was shot there." While I listened to my mother, I realized that Rousseau must have lived a long time ago and hoped that he had had a long life.

The couple arriving in Mexico.

I t was just as I thought. That big book was the most boring thing I'd ever read. It was not the sort of book to give an eleven-year-old boy like me, who would rather read comics than school books. But I stuck with it. Everybody was full of admiration at the way I spent a whole Sunday afternoon reading this big, complicated book.

I learned a lot from it, I have to say. Rousseau was the first "Sunday painter." People called him that because he had another job and didn't make his living from his painting. But he painted on other days of the week, of course. When he first started painting, everyone thought he painted badly, like a child. They said he was unable to create an illusion of depth in his canvases and he had no grasp of perspective. They were right, but that was the way Rousseau liked to paint the world, and when people laughed at his work it made him very sad.

"Clémence." Waltz with introduction for violin or mandolin. In addition to this piece, Rousseau wrote several theatrical entertainments, notably *The Vengeance of a Russian Orphan*, which was published by Tristan Tzara and is still occasionally performed today. Nonetheless, Rousseau was a better painter than he was a composer.

There was a moment when he thought about abandoning painting for music. He won a prize for his "Waltz for Clémence," which he played on the violin at a time when nobody was interested in his paintings. Fortunately, he stuck with painting, and now he is known the world over for his paintings, while nobody remembers his waltz.

Portrait of Rousseau by Delaunay, one of his true friends.

His first paintings, which were not popular, were not pictures of the jungle. Instead, he painted Parisian cityscapes with pedestrians, fishermen, and odd streets with doll-like figures.

Toward the end of his life, he turned to the jungle. It's a shame that he waited so long, because those pictures are the ones I like best. Rousseau, who socialized with "real" painters all week, spent most of his time with young artists who were interested in his unusual paintings. Some of the artists in this circle were to become famous, including Pablo Picasso, Robert Delaunay, Paul Gauguin, and Maurice Utrillo, as well as writers and poets like Alfred Jarry and Apollinaire.

Telegraph Poles at Malakoff.

The Bateau-Lavoir, or Boat-Laundry, in Montmartre, Paris, where several artists had studios. Picasso organized a banquet here in Rousseau's honor. It was on the latter occasion that Rousseau said to his host: "You and I are the two greatest painters in the world—you in the Egyptian style and I in the modern style."

The writer Alfred Jarry made Rousseau known in literary circles. He published articles about him in several magazines.

Rousseau knew he was a good artist, and he hoped to become rich and famous. Picasso and Delaunay sincerely admired his paintings, but certain false friends (bad painters all) laughed at him behind his back and played cruel jokes on him. One day one of them told him he'd been named to the Legion of Honor (a prestigious award in France). When he finally understood that it was a joke, he was so humiliated and sad that he cried. Rousseau retired early from his job to spend all his time painting, but his canvases didn't sell well, and often his only food was soup made by his best friend, a vegetable vendor. Fortunately, people in his neighborhood became proud of his talent. He even started to give painting lessons to neighbors and friends, first in an adult education school and then in his home.

But what interested me as I was reading this were his travels. Finally I came to his biography.

He was born on May 21, 1844, in Laval, Mayenne, in northwest France.

His studies—no, that didn't interest me.

In 1863 he stole 10 francs and some postage stamps from a lawyer for whom he was working. Not a good idea! He spent a month in prison. He enlisted in the army for seven years, and he was stationed in Angers, in western France.

I have a cousin in Angers. I went to see her the year before, and it certainly doesn't look like Mexico there. But back to the story. In fact, two battalions from Angers were sent to Mexico, but he wasn't in either of them. Later he told people that he *had* been sent to fight against the Mexicans. What a liar!

Portrait of Joséphine Noury, **Rousseau's second wife.**

In 1869 he married an eighteen-year-old dressmaker named Clémence, with whom he had nine children. Unfortunately, they all died young, except for a daughter, Julia. That must have made him sad.

He loved Clémence very much and wrote his waltz for her. After her death in 1888, he played it over and over, all alone in his studio.

Much later he married again to a woman named Joséphine-Rosalie, but she died three years later. Poor Rousseau!

Self Portrait.

In 1871 he was hired as a collector in a toll house in Paris. It was his job to make people pay their taxes. Not a popular job! Later, he told people that he'd been a customs officer. Another lie!

I read the rest as quickly as I could. There wasn't a trace of a voyage—he never even left Paris! On the other hand, I learned that he was arrested in 1907 for involvement in a scam and was given a two-year suspended prison sentence.

He died in 1910, at the age of 66.

What a story! What was I going to tell Caroline? When they tell us about the lives of great men and women at school, they always emphasize their good points: Napoleon's daring, Joan of Arc's courage, and Mozart's amazing gifts, which led to his playing the piano for kings when he was a child. None of them stole 10 francs from their boss!

When no one was looking, I skipped a few pages where I saw the phrases "complex oddness," "curving, divergent lines," and "Orphic Cubism."

Combat of a Tiger and a Buffalo, (1908).

Among all these complicated words, I came upon a phrase that astonished me. It was printed beside *Combat of a Tiger and a Buffalo*: "This brutal episode unfolds in absolute silence."

I looked at the picture more closely, and it was true: I had the impression that all was silence in the jungle surrounding these two beasts. It was almost as though their struggle occurred without any noise. But how can a painting be silent? (How can a painting be noisy, for that matter?) Very strange.

At the bottom of the page there was an image in black and white. I had a feeling I was about to discover something interesting about this Rousseau. Was I ever! Not only was he a liar, he was a common thief, too! The painting was a copy of a print by one Eugène Pirodon that was done earlier than Rousseau's canvas. And the drawing of the tiger was much better. But there were no plants. I had to admit that Rousseau painted terrific plants.

In fact, I came to realize that I liked the copy better than the "original." Not only because it was in color, but because of the thick network of all the leaves, fruit, and branches, and the dreamy look of the tiger. And then everything was eerily calm, like a dream.

The print by Eugène Pirodon, which appeared in the magazine *L'Art* in 1906.

I saw that he didn't stop at copying other painters, he also copied photographs. Just look at the monkey he put in a forest, or the zoo guard that he transformed into *Negro Attacked by a Jaguar*. But I don't think copying is the right word here. Since he'd never been to Mexico, or anywhere else except Angers, he had to find out how the jungle looked some other way. I asked myself where he got the ideas for his plants.

We were called to dinner. It was about time—I was getting tired. Caroline kept an eye on me all through the meal, but I kept my mouth shut. I didn't want to tell her anything until I'd finished the book.

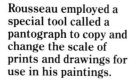

Rousseau employed a special tool called a pantograph to copy and change the scale of prints and drawings for use in his paintings.

Negro Attacked by a Jaguar.
The jaguar in this painting was modeled on a photograph in a children's book called *Wild Beasts,* published by a French department store called the Galeries Lafayette.

Tropical Forest with Monkeys, 1910.

Photograph from *Wild Beasts* used by the artist.

finally finished—now I knew everything about Rousseau the Customs Officer. I read all week, hiding from Caroline. I pretended to go to bed early each night, but in fact I read until it got too dark.

That's how I learned how Rousseau the Customs Officer—oops!—how Rousseau the Tax Collector managed to paint such wonderful plants and flowers without leaving Paris.

In fact, he was lucky, since he learned lots of things without ever going to school. He never studied painting, and yet, working on his own, he became a well-known painter. It was just the same with the plants. He never studied botany, but he taught himself about them by visiting the Museum of Natural History. This museum is in Paris and is also called the Plant Garden—an odd name: Have you ever seen a garden without plants? It's like a park, or an immense garden, with all kinds of trees and plants that are organized and identified.

The greenhouses at the Jardin des Plantes, or Plant Garden

In this garden there are exhibition halls with collections of minerals, stuffed animals, fossils, a small zoo, and greenhouses. Not greenhouses like the ones you see all the time for growing tomatoes, but GIGANTIC greenhouses, so high that whole trees—and tall ones, too —can grow in them. They're heated in winter so that plants from all over the world—Africa, Asia, and Aztec country—flourish as they do in their natural habitats, without realizing that they're in Paris.

hese greenhouses had already been built 100 years ago when Rousseau was alive, and he spent entire afternoons looking at the plants and making drawings. When he returned home, his head was so full of what he'd seen that he had no problems painting as though he were in the jungle. He said: "When I enter the greenhouses I become another man; it's as though I had entered a dream." So it's not so surprising that his paintings feel silent like some dreams do.

All I had to do now was pester my parents until they took me to Paris to see the Plant Garden there. While I was telling Caroline what I'd learned, Mom gave me a hard look:

"I know what you're up to! You're going to pester us until we take you to Paris to see the Plant Garden!"

And so we went. During the summer vacation, my parents took us to Paris. It was incredibly hot. The benches in the Plant Garden were crowded with people trying to rest a moment in the shade.

I'd been expecting to find some sort of open-air museum, but I was pleasantly surprised. The museum is more like a park, with a pool, statues, kiosks, and

people selling crepes and balloons. I found a terrifying statue of a man who'd been caught by a mother bear trying to steal her cubs; she's attacking him with claws and teeth bared, while he defends himself with a knife. It's sad, because clearly they're both going to die.

The big difference between this place and an ordinary park is that there are little signs on the trees with their names and countries of origin. It's surprising to see how some trees we take for granted have come from very far away. They have branches and leaves in every imaginable shape. Trees that were small when they were first planted there are now enormous. Comte Buffon, a famous scientist, planted a plane tree from the East here in 1785. You should see how big it is now!

The most amazing is the Ginkgo biloba (I took some notes), a rare tree from China that's 150 years old. It's a living fossil—its ancestors were already thriving 150 million years ago, at the time of dinosaurs.

Of course Caroline insisted on visiting the zoo. I told myself that Rousseau the Customs Officer walked through it before me, but it didn't help—I don't like to see animals in pens and cages.

The lions and bears were so hot they didn't move a muscle when Caroline roared at them, so she sulked.

Guide-promenade du jardin des plantes

But I quickly forgot about my sister, because we arrived at the greenhouses. They're not so different from the way they were in Rousseau the Custom Officer's day.

(You've noticed that, even though it makes my little sister happy, I call him Rousseau the Customs Officer instead of Rousseau the Tax Collector. That's because of my teacher at school. Before we left for summer vacation, we all had to make a presentation. We could choose our own subject. That wasn't a problem for me. I told her:

"Rousseau the Tax Collector."

"Who?"

"Rousseau the Tax Collector, the painter."

"Do you mean Rousseau the Customs Officer, or *le douanier* Rousseau?"

And I told her my little story.

She would have none of it. It was to be Rousseau the Customs Officer or nothing. I got so used to calling him "the customs officer" while writing my report that now I can't call him anything else.

Surprise!
When he painted this canvas, Rousseau had the impression his hand was being guided by another power, and he was a bit frightened of the tiger taking shape before his eyes.

As for my presentation, it was a huge success, especially when I imitated the tiger in the painting. The only problem was that I didn't have enough time to get through even half of what I'd prepared, so I had to present it to my friends over three recesses. But that was even better, because then I didn't have to worry about exaggerating a bit. What everybody really wanted to know about was Rousseau the Thief, and in that department I had to be inventive, because there wasn't much about it in the book. I know my friends: if I hadn't pretended he was a great thief, they never would have believed me when I told them he was a great painter!)

A jungle under glass.

The greenhouses were open only in the afternoon, so we were lucky. We bought tickets. Finally I was going to enter Rousseau's jungle! We went in. It was so hot! No wonder the plants thought they were in Mexico or Africa!

At first it really seemed like the jungle. Even the oddest trees outside in the park seemed like nothing in comparison with the ones in here: some were nothing but roots, others had leaves bigger than I was or trunks shaped like bottles. Some were smooth, some were twisted, some were hairy, and all of them were in a dense, vine-covered jungle worthy of Tarzan. We came to a small stream with turtles who dove into the water as we approached.

When Caroline saw the turtles she was tempted to step all over everything to pick one up, but I stopped her. I started to open my book, which I'd brought with me, but then I hesitated. There was something strange here, something that wasn't like the jungle at all. I suddenly realized what it was—the noise. In jungle movies there are all kinds of animal cries and exotic bird calls, but not here. It wasn't silent, far from it, but the only creatures that lived here were cooing pigeons and squabbling sparrows. That didn't make for a lot of local color. I would have preferred parrots, hummingbirds, and—why not?—snakes.

Exotic Landscape, 1910.

A sansevieria.

I opened the book at random to *Negro Attacked by a Gorilla*. I began to walk around the greenhouse, looking for a corner that reminded me of the picture. No luck. So I tried to find one of the big plants with orange flowers. I didn't see them, any more than I saw the bush with the huge leaves next to the Indian in another picture.

Disappointed, I turned to another picture, *Exotic Landscape* from 1910, with the monkeys. I looked for the big white flower on the right, but in vain. Could it be that this wasn't the right season?

Rousseau was inspired by flowers in the Plant Garden, but he felt free to work variations on them. This is a Nelumbo speciosum.

I went back to my *Combat of a Tiger and a Buffalo*. There I saw a tree I thought ought to be easy to find: a banana tree. I paced up and down the pathways without success, until I suddenly realized it was right beside me, by the entrance. There was no doubt about it—the sign on it said "banana." I looked at the painting, then at the plant, then at the painting, then at the plant. I was starting to wonder if Rousseau never even set foot in these greenhouses, any more than he had gone to Mexico! In the painting, the banana plant is a kind of tree, with a trunk, big leaves, and long branches with bunches of fruit at the ends. But the banana plant I had in front of me, the real one, wasn't like a tree at all—it didn't even have a trunk. It was more like a big herb plant, with leaves that stuck up rather than bending down. As for the small bunches of green bananas, they were close to the leaves, not at the end of a branch!

I was flabbergasted. Even the leaves were different. If you looked closely, you could see that they didn't have the fishbone veining pattern like the ones in the book.

BANANA
GENUS MUSA

After having made everyone think he was a customs officer and that he'd fought in Aztec country, this crazy guy said he'd spent time in greenhouses! Just like me, when I tell my parents I'm going to a friend's house to do my homework but play football instead. Where did he really go, I wondered, when he told everybody he was going to copy banana plants?

Banana plant (Musa sienesis).

I was tempted to throw the book to the turtles. Earlier, when my parents saw I was comparing the plants in the book with those in the greenhouse, they figured the project would keep me occupied for a while. So they left me alone and went to get something to drink with Caroline. No matter where you take her, before long she's hungry, or thirsty, or has to go to the bathroom.

Now nothing was keeping me from joining them, but instead I went to watch a painter I'd noticed earlier on. He was sitting on a folding stool with a big sketchbook on his knees and was drawing a pretty flower. At least this old guy was serious! You should have seen how carefully he reproduced every vein of every leaf and the least trace of pollen on a petal. I told myself I'd do better to spend my time studying artists like this one than jokers like Rousseau.

He caught sight of the book I still had under my arm.

"So you're interested in Rousseau the Customs Officer?"

What lousy luck. I dug in my heels.

"Not at all!"

He was surprised by my answer. He had watched me earlier, he said, and I had seemed quite interested. So I told him about the lies and the banana tree.

He smiled and closed his sketchbook.

"You're wrong. Rousseau often came here. When I say 'here,' I mislead you a bit. The greenhouse we're in now, called the Winter Garden, was built only in 1937. The one in Rousseau's time wasn't so tall, but it contained many of the same types of plants you see here now.

Waterlilies.

An Indian lotus.

A heliconia.

"I'm interested in capturing all the marvels of nature, but Rousseau was different. I'm sure that as soon as he came through the door he heard distant drums and the roars of the lions and tigers in his paintings. He must have been fascinated by all this green, too. When he painted at home, he felt suffocated by the jungle he'd invented and had to open his studio window to breathe.

"He had different palettes, each with several shades of a single color: all blues, all reds, or all greens. But it was green

Rousseau in front of one of his paintings.

that interested him the most. In a single one of his canvases one can count as many as 50 different shades. And he always started out by painting the plants, leaving a blank space for the human and animal figures which he filled in at the end."

The artist took the book from my hands and opened it as if he knew it by heart to the page of *The Dream,* which has two lions with strange eyes and a nude woman reclining on a sofa in the middle of the forest.

What an odd old man! Sometimes he spoke as though he were in a dream himself.

"But you draw better than him!" I said, determined to stand my ground.

He blushed. I guess he liked hearing me say that.

"Perhaps you're right, but surely you'd admit that, in the end, you prefer Yadwigha's strange dream to my little drawing."

I didn't know what to say because he was right.

Heliconia flowers surrounded by giant alocasia. These two plants inspired Rousseau, as did the cycads, the model for the palm-like plant in the center of the painting *The Merry Jesters*.

Fortunately, I heard someone calling me. It was my parents, who were at the entrance and were beginning to worry about me. Caroline was crying because she thought I was lost in the jungle forever. Then when she saw me, she stuck her tongue out at me. Caroline is like that. The old gentleman politely apologized for having kept me so long. He managed to con my parents into letting me stay with him a bit longer. He showed me a yucca plant so old that Rousseau might have touched it when he was a baby. Now it has a knotty, twisted trunk. He explained to me that plants from dry areas live the longest.

At least I saw one plant that might have inspired Rousseau: a cycad, which he put in all his paintings. On the other hand, he must have invented the big flower that looks like a lily of the valley, because it doesn't exist anywhere in the world.

After all the nice things he'd told me about Rousseau, the old gentleman complained that Rousseau always used the same plants in his paintings.

The Merry Jesters, 1906.

"I'm just an old nature lover. Nature invents so many forms and colors that I think it's the greatest of all artists. That's why I make do with reproducing its work. But Rousseau was different. He was a wondrous waking dreamer."

"A wondrous waking dreamer": Caroline liked that phrase when I told her Rousseau's real story. She tried to repeat it as fast as she could, got tongue-tied, and then burst out laughing.

We had more than a day left in Paris, and since I didn't want to leave without having seen some of Rousseau's paintings for real, I opened the big book to see where the ones I liked best were on display. What a disaster! The *Combat of a Tiger and a Buffalo* is in Cleveland, Ohio, the *Exotic Landscape* with the gorilla and the Indian is in Richmond, Virginia, *Yadwigha's Dream* is in New York City, and so is *The Sleeping Bohemian Girl. Storm in the Virgin Forest,* Rousseau's first jungle painting, is in London. I would have really liked to see the one entitled: *A Hungry Lion Attacks an Antelope and Devours it; a Panther Anxiously Awaits his Turn. Carnivorous Birds Have Ripped Pieces of Flesh from the Poor Animal, Who Sheds a Tear. Setting Sun.* Sometimes Rousseau used long titles to explain what was going on to people who didn't understand right away. And this *Lion* is in Switzerland! There are paintings in Philadelphia, Hamburg, Washington, Basel, Saint Petersburg, Moscow, Chicago, Los Angeles—and in two museums in Paris: the Louvre and the Orsay Museum. Only one of Rousseau's jungle pictures remains in the city where he painted them. Fortunately, it's one of the most beautiful ones (it was even on the cover of the big book) called *The Snake Charmer.*

A Hungry Lion Attacks an Antelope and Devours it; a Panther Anxiously Awaits his Turn. Carnivorous Birds Have Ripped Pieces of Flesh from the Poor Animal, Who Sheds a Tear. Setting Sun, 1905.

hen I told my parents we had to go to two more museums in Paris, they exclaimed "Oh no!" in unison, as if they'd been rehearsing it. They said we could only visit one, so I chose the Orsay Museum, because *The Snake Charmer* is there. I went to sleep that night thinking about the next day's encounter with the strange flute player in the moonlight.

I dreamed about the jungle. I got lost among the cycads and the fake banana trees. Caroline was adopted by a family of gorillas and swung from vine after vine. I tried to catch up with her to tell her she wasn't a real monkey, that she was a little girl who shouldn't hang from trees, scream all the time, and eat bananas with her toes. She just ignored me.

I met a terrifying tiger, but it was a motionless painted tiger. I tried to walk around it, but I always saw it from the same side, its yellow eyes following me, fierce and frightening.

Caroline woke me up by jumping from her bed onto mine and screaming.

"Caroline, stop acting like a monkey!" Mom shouted.

Surprise! (detail).
This painting was
Rousseau's first exotic
landscape. It was
exhibited in 1891.

he Orsay Museum is not an ordinary museum. In Rousseau's day it was a train station. Outside the entrance, statues of rhinoceroses, elephants, and monkeys put me in the right mood. Inside, it sure didn't look like a train station—it was more like a big, brightly lit temple. My parents wanted to wander around among the statues, but I had other things to do! I went up to a guard and asked her where the paintings by Rousseau were. The whole family followed me as I strode into a room to the side where all I saw was dark little landscapes. These were by Théodore Rousseau, a different painter who had nothing to do with Rousseau the Customs Officer. We headed for the upper floors. My parents had a hard time

This print brought Rousseau to the attention of Alfred Jarry.

keeping up with me, because Caroline was determined to play hide-and-seek behind the statues.

I entered a room by myself, and there it was, right in front of me—the snake charmer in her jungle of ten thousand different shades of green. When my parents arrived, I was up close, trying to imagine the old Rousseau's brush strokes from the old, cracked surface. Then I moved back and looked hard at the flutist's vicious, piercing eyes.

On another floor there were two paintings by Rousseau: an odd portrait of a stern looking woman and an allegory (that means a painting that represents an idea—Thanks, Dad!), a terrifying allegory of war. War is represented as a monstrous girl with sharklike teeth astride a crazy horse sticking out his tongue. Black birds eat the flesh of men's bodies lying on the ground, and the landscape is wasted as though a nuclear bomb had just exploded. It's as though Rousseau foresaw atom bombs. The horse looks more like a missile than a horse.

War.
When this painting was shown at the large annual exhibition of the Salon of Independent Artists, the painting bore the following legend: "She passes by sowing fright, leaving in her wake despair, tears, and ruin."

An illustration for the serial novel *The Czar*, published in 1889, that must have inspired Rousseau.

Rousseau's studio in
Paris.

I turned to my mother.

"How much does a painting like that
cost?"

"I don't know. A lot, millions."

"If his canvases are worth so much,
then why did he have to steal money?"

"They weren't worth that much when
he was alive."

A man beside us overheard our con-
versation. I had already noticed him because he had a little black goatee and
messy hair, and he looked a little wild.

"Madame," he said, "your son is ab-
solutely right. He's denouncing the art
market, and he has good reason. These
picture dealers wait like vultures for artists to die, then they get rich by selling
works by the same people they've al-
lowed to live and work in misery!" The
man was so angry I thought he might
swallow his goatee. I didn't understand
everything he said, but I had to agree it

wasn't fair for great painters to remain poor all their lives and then, after their deaths, for their canvases to earn millions of dollars for people who hadn't painted them. Finally the irritated man left the room and Mom let go a sigh of relief.

"Crazy!" she said.

But I don't think the man with a goatee was crazy. I think he was a painter, too. Of course he's angry that the dealers are waiting for him to die. If I were in his shoes I wouldn't be happy about it, either!

In any case, I'd only spent two days in Paris and I'd already met two artists! I couldn't wait to tell my friends. But I knew I'd have to exaggerate things a bit or else they wouldn't believe me.

he school year was about to start again, and that reminded me that I still hadn't decided what to do with my life.

Over the summer I had started painting jungle pictures, but I didn't want to be an artist, no sirree! Not if my pictures were going to sell for millions only after my death!

But I still enjoyed painting.

At this very moment I'm finishing my masterpiece. It's called *Exotic Landscape with Tiger, Caroline Dressed as a Customs Officer. Setting Sun.* The subject was Caroline's idea. I wanted to paint her as a jungle explorer, but she wouldn't pose unless I painted her as a customs officer. I've already filled up a big sheet of paper with drawings of the plants in the living room and a few other plants that I invented. The hardest thing was to get the cat to pose for my tiger—she clawed us three times! And of course Caroline was constantly hungry, or thirsty, or had to go to the bathroom. Maybe it would be best, when I grew up, to follow Rousseau's example and have a regular job, painting only in the evenings and on weekends.

Like Rousseau, I had to choose a profession to put with my last name, which was Vincent.

So what was it going to be? Vincent the Fireman? Vincent the Airplane Pilot? Vincent the Astronaut? Vincent the Quarterback? President Vincent? Vincent the Clown? Vincent the Businessman? Vincent the Frogman?

I couldn't make up my mind, and I sighed deeply.

enri Rousseau considered himself a great artist. In his own time people made fun of him and the "mistakes" in his paintings, but in the end he was proven right. It is a shame that people only realized how fine his work was after his death.

Although a unique artist, Rousseau is usually considered one of the primitive painters. He is perhaps the greatest artist in this category, but he was not the first.

In France, primitive painters, or painters with no formal art training, became common in the 19th century, at the beginning of the industrial era.

Until then, people who wanted to create beautiful objects could do so through the practice of a craft. A budding artisan entered a craftsman's guild (composed of furniture makers, stone cutters, blacksmiths, etc.), starting out as an apprentice, graduating to an intermediary level, and then after years of work, obtaining the official status of a master of their craft.

The goal of every worker was the completion of the masterpiece, or work considered worthy of a master, that would earn them this status.

With the coming of factory labor, such personal and original craftsmanship began to disappear. Laborers with a creative urge had to work on painting or poetry on their off hours, and so they never learned the basic skills involved. Such "Sunday artists" did not have the opportunity to study traditional paintings, so they invented their own means of expression. During work hours they had to stick by their machines or stay in their offices, but they spent their free time discovering their creative selves, which their regular work kept them from doing.

The word *primitive* is used to describe these painters because it reflects the simplicity, straightforwardness, and spontaneity that marks their work.

The United States has produced a great many primitive artists. Being a relatively new country, it did not have centuries of artistic tradition and history as did Europe. As a result, there was no one standard style taught to artists, as in most European countries, and it was easier for artists to express their visions of the world directly and spontaneously.

Penn's Treaty with the Indians, c. 1840, primitive painting by an unknown American artist.

By definition, primitive art is not affiliated with any school or tradition. Each artist working in this mode creates a highly personal style. Ferdinand Cheval, known as Cheval the Postman, is a particularly original example.

One day while delivering the mail, he came upon a rock that had been worked over by time and the weather. He thought it was beautiful, so he decided to collect and assemble such "natural sculptures" into an ideal palace in which all the cultures of the world would come together in perfect harmony.

For 25 years, he worked on his palace every day after making his rounds. On an outside wall of his castle he placed an inscription that sums up his ambition as a primitive artist: "Everything that you see is the work of a peasant. I have brought forth the queen of the world from a dream."

The Ideal Palace by Cheval the Postman.

GLOSSARY

affiliated: closely associated with another, usually in a dependent position

apprentice: one who is learning by practical experience the skill of an art or craft

Aztec: of or relating to the group of American Indians who founded a large empire in Mexico that was conquered by the Spanish in 1519

botany: the study of plant life

craftsmanship: skill in the manual arts

Cubism: a style of abstract art that shows several views of the same object at once and breaks objects down to their basic geometrical shapes

customs officer: one who collects duties and *taxes* on imported and exported products

cycad: a type of tropical plant that looks like a palm

denounce: to publicly proclaim as blameworthy or evil

douanier: a French word meaning "customs officer"

duty house: a place where *taxes* and *tariffs* are paid

exhibition: a public showing of art

goatee: a small, pointed beard on a man's chin

greenhouse: a glass structure used for the cultivation and protection of delicate plants

guild: a medieval association of craftsmen or merchants that often regulated working conditions and set prices

Orphism: an abstract artistic movement in which color is the dominant element of the painting

palette: the array of colors used by a particular painter

pantograph: an instrument, consisting of four rigid bars jointed in a parallelogram form, that is used to copy drawing and that can be adjusted to make the resulting copy larger or smaller than the original

perspective: the appearance to the eye of objects in respect to their relative distance and position

primitive painting: painting done by people with no formal art training and with no association to one particular school of art

spontaneity: the quality of being unrehearsed and unplanned

tariff: *taxes* on goods that travel in and out of a city

tax: a charge, usually of money, placed on people and property by their government

waltz: a style of music that accompanies a popular ballroom dance of the same name

Chronology

1844: Henri Rousseau is born in Laval, France.
1844–1861: Childhood in Laval.
1861: The family settles in Angers.
1863: Henri Rousseau works for an attorney. He and two of his colleagues are implicated in a petty theft. He enlists in the army.
1864: He is convicted of the theft and serves a month in prison, then resumes military service.
1868: Works as a bailiff's clerk.
1869: Marries Clémence Boitard.
1871: Rousseau's first son dies after only a few months of life. The couple later had eight more children, all but two of whom died very young, and only one, Julia Clémence, reached the age of 20. Rousseau works for the city of Paris as a toll collector.
1885: Settles in a studio at 16A Maine Cul-de-sac.
1886: Exhibits four works at the Second Salon of Independent Artists. From this point on he shows at every Salon.
1888: Clémence dies.
1893: Rousseau meets the writer Alfred Jarry.
1895: Completes his print *War*.
1899: Completes his musical play *The Vengeance of a Russian Orphan*. Marries Joséphine Noury.
1901: Begins to teach painting and drawing.
1903: Death of his second wife.
1906–1907: Meets the poet Guillaume Apollinaire and the painter Robert Delaunay.
1908: Begins to organize "musical and familial" gatherings in his home at which neighbors and students can meet his artist friends. Banquet at the Bateau-Lavoir.
1910: Dies from a gangrene infection in his leg.

Where are Rousseau's Paintings?

Cover and pp. 24, 39: *Combat of a Tiger and a Buffalo,* The Cleveland Museum of Art, gift of the Hanna Fund.

P. 8: *The Snake Charmer,* Orsay Museum, Paris.

P. 9: *Exotic Landscape,* collection of Mr. and Mrs. Paul Mellon, Upperville, Virginia.

P. 10: *Myself, Landscape Portrait,* National Gallery, Prague.

P. 11: *The Toll House,* London, Courtauld Library.

P. 13: *The Muse Inspiring the Poet,* Museum of Art, Basel.

P. 19: *Soccer Players,* Guggenheim Museum, New York.

P. 20: *The Telegraph Poles in Malakoff,* private collection, Berne.

P. 22: *Portrait of the Artist's Wife,* Paris, Louvre, Picasso Bequest.

P. 23: *Portrait of the Artist by Lamplight,* Paris, Louvre, Picasso Bequest.

P. 26: *Negro Attacked by a Jaguar,* Museum of Art, Basel.

P. 27: *Tropical Forest with Monkeys,* Mr. and Mrs. John Hay Whitney collection, New York.

P. 33, 47: *Surprise!,* National Gallery, London.

P. 36: *Exotic Landscape,* The Norton Simon Foundation, Pasadena.

P. 42: *The Dream,* Museum of Modern Art, New York.

P. 45: *The Merry Jesters,* Philadelphie Museum of Art, Arensberg collection.

P. 47: *A Hungry Lion,* private collection, Basel.

P. 51: *War,* Orsay Museum, Paris.

Photographic Credits

Cleveland Museum of Art: cover & pp. 24, 39.

Mellon Collection, Upperville, Virginia: 9.

Norton Simon Foundation, Pasadena: 36.

Museum of Modern Art, New York: 44.

Philadelphia Museum of Art: 45.

Musee National d'Art Moderne, Paris, c Sabam, Brussels: 20 left.

Reunion des Musees Nationaux, Paris: 22, 23.

Lauros-Giraudon: 8, 50, 56, 57.

Giraudon: 10, 13.

Artephot/M. Babey: 20 bottom, 47.

Artephot/Held: 11 right, 15 top.

Harenberg Kommunikation: 14.

Viollet Collection: 15 right

Harlingue-Viollet: 15 bottom.

Roger-Viollet: 19, 21 right.

Sipa-Press: 21 left.

Hinz: 26.

Bridgeman/Artephot: 33, 47.

Lavaud/Artephot: 27.

Y. Delange: 28, 34, 36 bottom, 37, 39 right, 41, 44.

Sirot-Ziolo: 53.

P. Trela-Ziolo: 56.

F. De Boeck: 58–59.